PRICE IT TO SELL & PROFIT KNOW YOUR VALUE & CHARGE YOUR WORTH

NICHELLE WOMACK, MBA

DEDICATION

This book is dedicated to all the hard-working boss women
who purposely make it happen every day.

CONTENTS

ACKNOWLEDGMENTS

Business is always scary, time consuming and full of risk. When you find someone who believes in you and helps you create that vision, that makes all your hard work possible. I would never have come this far without God, my husband, my two boys and my parents. They've always been the backbone of my success. Their inspiration and motivation to push me when I wanted to quit has kept me level headed and even more determined to move forward with every dream that I desire to achieve. Thank you family for being my rock.

This book is for the small business owner seeking to strategically price their products for sale without feeling guilty. Your products or services are the cornerstone of your business. No one goes into business just to say they are in business. Most go into to business to profit and profit over and over again. Therefore, in order to create and operate a profitable business, you must price your products and/or services for sale. This book will give you tips, strategies, formula's and a plan for consistent profitability. If you are needing assistance with growth strategies and business building tactics, learn more with The Start, Market and Grow Business Bundle.

1

THE CHEAPEST PRICE MAY NOT BE THE BEST PRODUCT

My momma used to say, "you get what you pay for." As I've gotten older and I'm spending my own money, I believe that to be true. Yes.. I want a bargain. And yes.. I want to save money. But I also want a quality product or service. Just because it's cheap doesn't mean it will do what you need it to do. Chances are you don't always buy the cheapest product either. There are a number of reasons to take "price" this into consideration when creating products or services for your target audience. Let's discuss a few.

The Psychology of Shopping

People buy out of need, desire or want. Buying also has a lot to do with how a person is feeling, how they view what they are buying and what they have been taught. In some cases, buying the cheaper product or service is logical if it is a quality item on sale and/or you have a coupon. Price and the perception of value are not the same thing. There are different things which influence this perception. Just because it's expensive doesn't mean that it is worth it. Value is based on worth. Is it a worthy investment for the short term or long term? When pricing your product, consider this. Will your clients get value in it for days, weeks or even years to come? If so, sell it as such.

Emotional Shopping

Bottom line.. people are emotional. Women have been noted as being so. Women are also the primary decision makers when buying. Emotions enter purchasing decisions a lot more than most business owners might think. Studies have shown that consumers buy based on emotion and then try to justify their choice with logic, not the other way around. This can lead people to spend more than they can afford. The emotional attachment to things based on appearance or desire can cause one to buy and regret later. These emotions can cause some people to buy things they really don't need because they want to "keep up with the Joneses". Therefore, you want to express why your product or service will help them and won't be a regretted problem later down the road.

Choice Support

The emotions that caused a person to buy in the first place can keep them coming back for more, a phenomenon known as choice support. This is what you want. This process triggers people to become repeat customers. Once they have purchased from you, they will continue to do so to "prove" they made the right choice in the first place. You want to keep these customers happy always. They may even refer because they are so happy creating more profits for you in the long run.

Branding

Brands drive buying power. Everyone wants to be associated with the best and the latest. In essence, branding is a shortcut for shoppers. Coke versus Pepsi, Wendy's versus McDonald's... we all have individual tastes and preferences and buying by brand ensures we get what we want no matter what it may cost. It can also be associated with quality, such as a designer dress or shoes. Branding is a power statement! If you got it, flaunt it. Big business thrives on creating a branding experience that customers will remember and most have succeeded. For example, think Timex versus Rolex and you will understand that some people buy luxury brands because of the name, quality and prestige of owning them.

Brand Loyalty

If they are loyal, they will be on your buying list forever. This is the type of customer you want. At this stage, you've hit the goldmine. Choice support is one of the reasons for brand loyalty. It is not just about the name on the label. It is also an "easy button" that tells busy people they will get their money's worth and/or get what they will like and need by doing business with that brand. These types of supporters are committed to you and you only until or unless you prove them wrong. Again.. keep them happy. They will be your biggest and greatest cheerleaders in business.

Price versus Value

Price and value have a common distinction. An expensive car like a Range Rover is prized because of the brand, the "wow" factor and the envy factor. A person who owns one will feel proud of the purchase and be happy to show it off. They will also be eager to dangle it in front of other people to arouse their envy and curiosity. If we think about it, Nissan, Toyota and Lexus are all made by the same company. But it is the perception of value that drives Lexus sales. No matter the price, the value of high class, distinguishes this type of customer from everyone else. To make this point ever clearer. If your price is low, you may not get the type of buyer you desire and vice versa. Therefore, it is so important to know who your customer is, what they need from you and how can you deliver it at a price they desire.

Ethical Considerations

Ethics should always be the practice of your business. Ethical considerations are the beliefs and values in the minds of the consumers and in relation to the company as a whole. This drives sales. People are willing to pay more for organic food, for example, or items they feel are healthier or more ethically produced, such as grass-fed beef without any antibiotics, or non-GMO foods. When a consumer knows the company cares about their well-being, they are more inclined to support the brand, product or service.

People buy "green cleaning products" at a higher price than popular commercial brands because the perception is they are healthier and the person is doing their part to help the environment. Some people will only buy products with a Made in the USA label. Or they pay more for a hybrid version of the same car in order to support their personal values. Personal values are taught, learned or achieved through buying power.

Understanding the psychology of shopping and using it to craft your offers can help you increase your sales and profits tremendously.

2

THE PSYCHOLOGY OF PRICING RIGHT

Psychology is the scientific study of the mind and behavior. How a customer thinks and buys is psychological. As it relates to sales and profits, psychological pricing is a pricing and sales strategy used based upon the belief that certain prices will influence a potential customer in one or more ways. Psychological pricing is designed to help remove the resistance of making a purchase. As a result, the company can make more sales. Large companies like Amazon use psychological pricing to drive sales. But small businesses can use it too once they master the basic concepts. Listed below are several influencing factors that can help you sell and make a profit with your target audience.

Nines and Sevens

The next time you go in a store, pay attention to the pricing. There's something about a 9 and a 7. As odd as it may seem, $99.99 or $99.97 is psychologically more enticing and acceptable than $100. For some reason, the human mind zones in on the first 9, not equating it with the higher price of $100, which is more accurate. The power of "9" at the end or beginning seems cheaper in the mind at least. When pricing your products or services, consider this.

The Appearance of Discounting

Everybody likes a sale and many people will look for a low price or a big discount. Listing a much higher price and then giving a discount can attract the bargain shopper. The illusion that they are getting what you have to offer a great price will entice them to spend and possibly buy more. However, make certain that you are strategic in the process. Don't do it regularly. Do it when least expected so it doesn't become over used. Customers sometimes like mystery. It's intriguing!

Give Away Coupons

Everyone likes the feeling of getting a good deal. There's something about a coupon that brings out the kid in an adult. In fact, couponing has become a skill and a hobby. Coupons attract the bargain hunters. It's a win both for the customer and you as the business owner. You only have to offer the big discount to the people who use the coupon and not to everyone who comes to your site. Or you can save the coupon offer for new customers or customers who buy often. There's so much you can do with a coupon offering. Make certain to include it in your pricing strategy and marketing.

Price Alignment

A coupon is useful too because you don't want to price your product too low in the marketplace or else consumers might think it is inferior or that there is something wrong with it. How many times have you saw a low-priced item and asked the store clerk, "Is something wrong with it?" Your customers will do the same if everyone else is higher and you are significantly lower. Pay attention to what your competition does and how they structure their pricing. Your prices need to be roughly in line with the top products that are already selling in your niche or industry.

Price versus Value

Price vs value... Not everyone will buy the lowest priced item. Some people like to buy high end products and services. Keep these clients in mind when structuring your prices. If you are going to price yourself higher than the other items in the marketplace, you need to have a clear value proposition as to why your item is better. Have specific and key points to distinguish them. I like the good, better and best structure. If we think of Nissan, Toyota and Lexus, they are all made by the same company. Essentially, a car is a metal box with wheels and an engine designed to get you from A to B. But the Lexus commands a higher price tag. It conveys quality, style and comfort. It can also reflect success because a person is able to afford it.

Bundling

People like to buy things in sets or a combination of things that are related. The aspect of bundling helps boost the per-customer value while still permitting them to believe that they are getting a great deal. Amazon does this all the time with their bundling suggestions underneath the main product on each sales page. A bundle can save money if the total price adds up to considerably less than all the items priced individually if the prices on the items are competitive. However, this is not always the case. So, pay attention to what you are offering when using this strategy.

When buying ink cartridges, for example, a bundle of all the colors needed would be good value if the total is considerably less than what you would pay separately for four cartridges. If the overall price is cheaper than in most stores, a person is more than likely to buy it. Comparison shopping could help the consumer determine if it were the best deal. Nevertheless, consumers often buy bundles for the sake of convenience and ease. It takes the guesswork out of the issue of what they really need and psychologically, they are happy because they feel they have gotten a bargain. And who doesn't like a bargain.

As a small business owner, you should take the time to master the various psychological pricing strategies and see what a difference they can make to your bottom line and profit potential.

3

PLAYING WITH THE NUMBERS WHEN PRICING YOUR PRODUCTS

Numbers matter and cents count. Pay attention to your pricing strategies and understand how this simple fact can change your business forever. What's the difference between $99.99 and $100? More than a penny, it turns out, when it comes to psychological pricing strategies.

What Is Psychological Pricing in Detail?

If you don't leave with anything else from this book, remember this. Psychological pricing is a pricing and sales strategy based upon the belief that certain prices will influence a potential customer in one or more ways. Psychological pricing is designed to help remove resistance to making a purchase, so the company can make more sales.

One of the most influential factors are the numbers you use.

The Numerical Value of 9

Studies have shown that the most successful marketing numbers are 9 and 7. It might not seem like it, but there can be a huge difference between $99.99 and $100. People tend to identify with the lower amount of $99 even though the price is nearly $100, and they are therefore more willing to buy.

Have you ever noticed the products being sold on TV for only $19.99? These are 9s at work in several ways. The number 9 is attractive because it is under $20. Customers don't really pay attention to the "Plus shipping and handling part," although they should.

The hypnotizing factor of 9 can change and elevate your sales strategy.

These special deals also come with a ", But you can get a second set free if you act now," offer. The terms of the offer state, "Just pay shipping and handling."

These marketers are strategic, and they know exactly how much people need to spend for the company to turn a profit. By using 9s, they are removing price resistance and opening the door to more sales. The second item free shows that the price of the item is going to be low if the cost of shipping and handling will cover it. That "free" item needs to be paid for somehow.

The Value of 7

The second most popular number is 7. It is also good for this type of pricing, such as $99.97. It also works well for round numbers without cents. For example, the typical pricing structure you will see for eBooks, products and services will be based around 7s, including $7, $17, $27, $37, $47, $67, $77 and $97, rather than $9, $19, and so on.

You will also see $197, $297, $497, and $997 rather than $199, $299 and so on. If you are not going to add cents to your price, make your number something with a 7.

Strikethroughs to Stimulate Sales

This task works well with online marketing. When pricing your product, be sure to check your competition to see what they are charging for a similar item. Set your price slightly higher. Then use a strikethrough or cross out the higher price and insert a lower one. This will make them feel they are getting better value. Set the price at $97, then strike it through and show a price of $77.

Discounts to Stimulate Sales

Cost vs profit is a formula that needs to be mastered. It is essential that you know the production cost of every item you sell. Then calculate the amount of discount you can offer to make a profit on the item. Use the strikethrough technique and a red price to call attention to your "rock bottom offer" of only $39.99 or $37.

By knowing the power of your numbers, you will increase your sales immediately and make profits.

4

WHEN AND WHY SHOULD YOU OFFER SOMETHING FOR FREE?

For too many business owners, the word "free" strikes terror into their hearts. Yet giving away free items can be a good way to stimulate sales for several reasons. "Free" should only be scary if that's all you do. The intent is to offer great "free" and fabulous "paid." If you focus on offering your best product and/or service, the "free" won't mean anything in the long run. In fact, free gives a sample of what it is and why they should buy. Listed below are several reasons why "free" should be a part of your marketing strategy.

Getting People on Your Email Marketing List

If you've never heard the saying, "the money is in the list. Believe it, the money is in the list." This is what many "gurus" will forget to tell you. Without a list as a small business owner, you will probably not sell anything or be in business long. If I had known that when I started my business 25 years ago, God knows where my business would be. The significance of email marketing should not be taken for granted. It is the bread and butter and the lifeline of small business. Email marketing list building is important because your list can be an effective marketing tool. Every time there is something new in your business, you have a list of people eager to learn more and more than likely buy. If you haven't started, get a list, build it, grow it and nurture it now!

The best way to get customers on your list is to offer them something for free such as an eBook or an eCourse. It is a "bribe", but also a free sample that shows the quality of your work and your expertise in your niche.

After you deliver, then market to them regularly. This is not spam, but permission-based marketing at its best. Don't spam! You will lose your customers respect, more than likely get blocked and maybe even reported to the FCC. Remember... build relationships not enemies.

Your Email Marketing

Research shows that emails with the word **"free"** in the subject line are opened more often than those that don't. However, don't overuse the word as it can also trigger spam filters on some email services.

A Free Sample

Be careful how you use the free sample. The free item is the quality of the product you have to offer. If you have ever been in a supermarket where representatives are handing out samples, you'll understand the value of free. No one wants to buy a large package of something without knowing that it tastes good. Therefore, your "free" should be so enticing that you have them crawling and begging for more. Basically, when they can't get enough of you, you will always be on their mind when they are in need for what you have to offer.

A Loss Leader as a Lure

"Free" also counts as a loss leader. Supermarkets offer good bargains each week to get people into the store based on the assumption once they are there, they will than likely buy more than just the item on sale. The hope is that their cart will be full of other stuff as well. As a small business owner, this is your hope as well. Keep your store well stocked with plenty of good items so purchasing will not be a problem.

Reciprocity

Reciprocity is so key in business. When you give away something for free, you've done them a favor. As a result, they feel they owe you and are more willing to buy as well as share what they bought with others if they are happy.

A Thank You to Loyal Customers

People have forgotten the simple task of being thankful. "Free" items can also be used as a thank you for being a loyal customer. Studies have shown that 80% of a business's sales come from 20% of their customers. "Free" can lure new customers, but it can also keep your existing customers coming back for more.

Promotional Items

Everyone loves promo items. Especially when they are cool. Use it to your power, business recognition and growth. "Free" items given away at trade shows, conferences, charity events and so on create the perception your company is worth doing business with. People like to associate with a brand, remember. Handing out pens and other useful items gives you a better chance of participants remembering you when they get home. They will also have no problem spreading the word because your pen might get passed along. Promo items are powerful, and they are around when you aren't. Get them and use them.

Coupons

Who doesn't like saving money? People love saving money and coupons are a popular way to give things away or deeply discount them. A 100% off one-time use coupon costs nothing to make, but it can help promote sales easily because it removes the risk of buying from you. Especially if they don't know you. Risk-free is a powerful psychological incentive too.

Bonus Items

One of the most effective strategies in online marketing is "free "bonus items. For example, if a company is selling digital products such as eBooks, multimedia courses, and so on, they can make the main product seem more attractive by offering additional bonus items such as cheat sheets, checklist, and so on. Everybody likes a bonus.

All these tips will increase the perceived value of your products and/or services. Even if it is the same price (or more) than that of your competition. It's an incentive to do business with you. Your bonuses should be unique, and again, reflect your expertise and why they should buy more. Free really can lead to sales if the item is of high quality and reflects well on your business. Don't take "free" for granted. Use it to your advantage and your profits.

5

IT'S A LIMITED TIME OFFER. GET IT NOW!

Time is a commodity that can never be returned. The clock is ticking and will keep ticking regardless of if you acknowledge it or not. You have only 10 minutes to decide whether to buy an item. Or, it's a Gold Box offer at Amazon, and the item will only be available today, or while supplies last.

If you've ever seen these types of offers online, they are what are termed limited time offers (LTOs), and they are a psychological pricing strategy that works every time for several reasons.

What Is a Limited Time Offer?

An LTO is an offer that is good for only a short amount of time, and then it is gone forever, maybe. You can use LTOs in your online business to drive sales. This method will keep your customers on their toes and yearning for more. You can even add a countdown clock to your sales pages to reinforce the perception that time is running out and they don't want to miss such a great deal. This simple strategy can elevate your sales within a matter of minutes and hours down to the final second.

Why do LTOs work so well? Here are a several reasons.

Bargain Hunting

Who doesn't like a bargain? People trample over people to get the best deal. At least during "Black Friday" they do. Some people just can't resist a bargain. Giving them an LTO, especially if your customer has had their eye on that product, is a win for both of you. You get the sale and they get the product.

Scarcity

When demand is low, product is available. When demand is high, it is scarce. The limited nature of the offer implies scarcity. It could be a small number of items available only for that short time as well as the tight timeline. People who don't want to miss out really need to act fast and believe me they do. Using this method to secure sales will earn you an extra few dollars. Big retailers do it all the time and they are still in business. So, don't feel bad. It's business, not personal.

Exclusivity

This kind of goes hand and hand with branding. People like to be attached to the exclusive and want to say they are the only ones who were able to get it. Make an exclusive offer. You can even sweeten the deal with an LTO that has never been offered before and won't be offered again. For example, you could create a bundle of your top products all for one low price as an LTO. Another Ching Ching.

You might also offer a pre-launch special for a new product, with the clock ticking down until launch day, when the full price will go into effect. This is usually a very attractive offer and a reward of sorts for those who are on your email marketing list. It offers them an exclusive no one else will get and they feel supper special. My favorite quote, "people don't care how much you know until they know how much you care." This simple strategy will show your customers that they are very special and just because.. they get the exclusive.

Fear of Missing Out

No one wants to be left out. One of the reasons why an LTO works so well is the fear of missing out. They don't want to have to pay more at a future date. They might even be afraid that they will never see the product, or the sale price, or the exclusive offer, ever again. This right here is a super diamond worth holding on to forever.

Fear of Loss Rather Than the Joy of Gain

In terms of what is called psychological pricing, studies have shown that consumers are motivated more by a fear of loss, of missing out, than they are by the joy of gain. eBay's slogan used to be "Shop victoriously," which referred to the auction aspect of the site and putting in the winning bid to secure the item. However, as eBay began to sell more items at the "Buy Now" price than at auction. They eventually dropped the slogan. The joy of gain and of winning were no longer the key motivating factors for shopping there. It was the fear of missing out, especially on limited quantity items, and losing out by a cent or two on the auction at the last minute. eBay is still making massive profits with this strategy.

Now it's your turn as a small business owner to put these strategies to work. Which one will you incorporate first? Remember... it won't work if you don't do it. Nevertheless... have a plan and then execute.

If you're not already using LTOs in your marketing mix, try one and see how you can boost your sales and profits.

6

Gender-Based Price Discrimination

In terms of psychological pricing, one more important pricing strategy to be aware of, both as a consumer and a business person, is gender-based price discrimination. Discrimination is any order is out of order and it should not be a form of practice in any aspect. Yet, it does exist. Listed

What Is Gender-Based Price Discrimination?

Gender-based price discrimination can be defined as companies or services charging different rates to women versus men for no other reason than the fact that the customer is a woman. This so-called "pink tax" has been around since the 19th century, when women's hats and gloves were taxed more than a man's.

Over the years, gender-based price discrimination has become an increasingly common strategy amongst business owners, leading women to pay an average of 7% of more for goods and services, even though in some areas of the US this is illegal.

Gender-Based Price Discrimination in Retail

Women's products tend to be higher priced than men's. Studies have shown that the exact same toiletries as a man's are priced 25% higher when put in a pretty package. Women's designer clothes and accessories are significantly higher priced than, for example, a man's suit or pair of shoes.

Women are so used to paying more that they don't really reflect on the issue. However, one study showed that they are paying an average of around $1,400 more annually, which over their lifetime can add up to a significant waste of cash they could have put into a retirement account or used towards immediate expenses.

This issue becomes even worse if you consider the fact that many women earn one-third to one-half less than men simply because they are a woman. Pay equality is starting to improve, but women don't get a 33%

discount off their food, rent, electricity and so on. With more than 50% of all US households being headed by women, gender-based price discrimination can have a significant impact on the children as well. It ends up being tougher and tougher to make ends meet on a smaller salary with more costly products and services.

Women as the Shoppers in the Household

Even if a woman has a domestic partner, recent statistics show that women do around 90% of the shopping or make 90% of the major shopping decisions in a household, even buying the men their clothes and weighing in heavily on what were once "male-oriented products" such as cars. We can see the shift if we look at car ads, which now include women and children in the ads to connect with female customers.

Women Buying Services

Women are also asked to pay more for basic services, such as going to the hairdresser or getting their clothes dry cleaned. One study conducted by CBS news showed women were paying more for the same shirts because, the owners claimed, "Women's clothes have to be handled differently than men's because the pressing machines are designed for men's shirts only."

It is important to note that in New York City, certain cities in Florida, and in California, charging more for services is illegal.

Gender-Based Pricing in Your Business

More and more states are cracking down on this problem as legislation continues to make great stride in correcting this issue. Don't be a victim to this practice. Be fair in your pricing and never get caught up in discrimination one way or the other. It's totally not right nor fair.

7

SEVEN TIPS TO INFLUENCE THE CUSTOMER'S PERCEPTION OF PRICE

There are several ways to influence your target customer's perception of price so they feel they are getting a good deal. Listed below are the key influencing tactics with price.

9s and 7s

I know this has been repeated several times, but it is so key when pricing your products or services. 99 cent stores are hugely successful with this strategy. Any number with a 9 in it seems to work like magic. $9.99 works better than $10. People identify with the first number they see, so they feel the price is closer to $9 than to $10. For online products, 7 as a round number works effectively, such as $7 for an eBook, $47 for an eCourse and so on. These numbers can be used in conjunction with what is termed anchor pricing.

Anchor Pricing

With anchor pricing, you show the "real value" of the item and then the retail price. It creates the perception that the consumer is getting a huge bargain. For example, if you say the value is $127, but they can buy the item today for only $27, that removes a lot of price resistance.

Making the deal a special one that will only last for a limited time will also affect their perception. In marketing terms, people are more motivated by the idea of loss, of missing out on a great deal, than they are of gaining something, so the "urgency" factor of a limited time offer (LTO) is more likely to make them hit the Buy button.

Stacking Value

When it comes to pricing, your first reference point should be the prices that your competitors are charging for a similar product. Then you can "stack" the value of your offering; that is, add extras that are valuable and unique to your business.

8

TEN PRICING TIPS FOR OFERING SPECIAL OFFERS

Ten Pricing Tips for Special Offers

There are numerous ways to construct special offers that will boost your sales considerably once you've mastered them. Listed below are 10 that I've used in my business throughout the year. You can use one or a combination. You will also see that I reiterate a couple over again.

Holiday Sales

Almost every business offers a holiday sale at least a couple of times a year. These are attractive offers on things that a person might need, being offered at a competitive price. They can increase profits by encouraging the person to buy more, because they feel they are getting good value.

Special Occasion Sales

These are driven by certain events, such as back to school or graduation or home improvements/spring cleaning. Some of the items will be on sale, but others are at full price, or perhaps even higher than that of the competition.

Loss Leaders

These are very low-priced products that are used as a lure to get people in the store in the hope they will buy more. Just look at the bargains in your local supermarket or department store flyer and you will see how well this strategy can work.

Limited Offer

If you look in the flyer and see "Limit one per customer," you will also see the limited offer strategy in action. This not only encourages one to buy, it encourages them to send other people to buy too.

Limited Time Offer (LTO)

Supermarket flyer prices are good for only a week. Then they are gone forever. You can use LTOs in your online business to drive sales. You can even add a countdown clock to your sales pages to reinforce the perception that time is running out and they don't want to miss such a great deal.

One-Time Offer (OTO)

You can also use OTOs in your online business. This means that they will see the offer one time only, and never again. It is a way of driving demand. It is also a way to increase the initial value of a customer once they have bought from you, with the OTO being like a bonus to thank them. An OTO will usually be at a deeply discounted price that they would be foolish to refuse.

Upsells

Upsells are another type of special offer to help drive sales. Assume a customer has already bought your main product. The upsell is a second product that is bigger and better than your main product, and therefore more expensive. Think silver, gold and platinum packages, or a deluxe edition at a great price. This can drive profits up tremendously. This should be a regular strategy in your business building portfolio.

Downsells

A downsell will be similar to the upsell, but not have as many components to it, and therefore not be as expensive. It would be like the silver package rather than the platinum. It should contain the most important part of the upsell for a lower price, but still be potentially higher than the main product's price. This is the middle of the road product for those customers with a little more to invest, but not enough to the best. Still.. make certain it's worth having.

Fire Sales

A fire sale is an "everything must go" type of sale. You should only run these a maximum of twice a year. It's a good way to make money from any products that are not selling well or products which you would like to either discontinue, or just want to boost sales to get rid of overstock. Fire sales should be a limited time offer, such as 72 hours. Make it enticing an exciting.

Bundles

e. Everyone's needs are not the same.

Small business owners often believe that by putting the price on the page, they are creating a lot of work for themselves in the long run because they will have to change the price each time they want to increase the price or run a new offer. However, this does not have to be the case. It is possible to make it easy on yourself if planned appropriately. Run your sale, then swap back the numbers when the sale is over.

You can also use PayPal as your accepted payment collection service and put the price right on the button. Name each button according to the product. As soon as you change the price in PayPal, it will update your sales page. Swap the price back when your sale is finished. Sam Cart is another vehicle to use this pricing strategy.

The Bottom Line

A lot of marketers wait until the prospective customer have read a significant portion of the sales letters before adding the "Buy Now" button or link and the price. By doing this, the prospect will have read through the many features and benefits and feel increasingly eager to buy. When the image of the item and the "Buy Now" button or link appear together, it's only natural for them to click.

Red Marks the Spot

Some marketers put the price in red to call attention to it. Studies have shown that men tend to favor prices in red. Red prices stand out more and when next to the Buy button, seem to make it quite logical to click and buy.

Bundling

One way to increase the value of each customer yet avoid "sticker shock" at the same time is to bundle several of your popular products and services together into one great package deal. For example, you could sell a small library of short eBooks for $17, instead of trying to sell each one individually for $7 each.

If you are a virtual assistant, you could offer ten blog posts on a topic at 500 words each, plus uploading it into WordPress and optimizing it for the search engines, for $147, instead of just $97 for the blog posts.

A good marketing website should contain content that influences your target customer to decide immediately. By including prices on your website, you take the guesswork out of buying from you and increase the know, like and trust factor that is essential in building sustainable business relationships.

10

THE SECRET OF AMAZON'S PRICING STRATEGY AND HOW YOU CAN MASTER IT TOO

S o finally, let's talk about the big elephant in the room, Amazon. It's no secret that it is one of the most successful businesses of our time. Mr. Bezos started in a garage selling books and now has grown his business to over a billion dollars making him a very rich man as of 2018. When you are worth a billion dollars and you grew from nothing to something, you deserve the respect.

Let's look at the sales model of Amazon. Amazon's sales are more than one trillion dollars annually. How have they managed to become so successful is the big question many aspiring and existing entrepreneurs want to know.

Their secret is psychological pricing. There are numerous techniques Amazon uses that are worth considering in your own business if you want to be more competitive and grow exponentially. You never know, you could be next.

Amazon uses numerous strategies when they are setting their prices. But as you can imagine, they have several other tricks up their sleeves as well. Let's dive into some popular strategies that keep them successful.

Discounting

Amazon will discount popular products but boost the price on less popular ones. In this way, they create the perception that they offer good prices on everything, which is of course not always the case.

Loss Leaders

They will also create loss leaders; that is, items they are willing to sell cheaply to get people to buy other items. They will offer deep discounts in their Gold Box offers, which act as a lure to get people to shop and buy more.

"Let's Have a Sale" Sales

Amazon will invent a reason for a sale. They can be tied to the holidays, or for no reason at all other than to stimulate sales. Often, these sales are limited time offers (LTOs) - items on sale for only a short time. This psychological pricing strategy is based on people not wanting to miss out on a great deal. The Gold Box items are on sale, but the clock is ticking, and the quantity might run out.

Recommendations

Amazon's recommendations to you are based on your previous purchasing history, but while those items might be attractive, they are not usually discounted. However, Amazon is relying on its reputation as a reliable seller with good customer service as the means of getting you to buy even if they don't offer rock-bottom prices.

Free Shipping, and Prime

You also get free shipping in some cases. Prime membership entitles you to both free shipping and other perks like TV shows, music and audio books, for one low annual price. Studies have shown that Prime members spend a significant amount more each year than those who are not. Therefore, Amazon wins again.

Bundling

Bundling groups two or more products together for a discounted price compared to what you would pay separately. It may seem like a good deal, but beware. When it comes to electronics, for example, Amazon might lure you with a great price on a flat-screen TV, but the accessories they offer such as headphones, cables and so on, are not competitively priced at all. You could do much better if you shopped around. However, many people like the convenience of one price for all and will gladly pay for a bundle and think they got a bargain.

The sales and marketing staff at Amazon are pros when it comes to selling and have built up their impressive business in only a few short years starting completely from scratch. Study their psychological pricing methods and see which make sense and apply it to your business. Then watch the sales flow in. Amazon has mastered it and you can too.

ABOUT THE AUTHOR

Nichelle Womack is a serial entrepreneur, mom, wife, small business consultant, author and real estate boss. She has been a business owner for a little over 25 years.

Nichelle has worked in multiple areas of corporate America in numerous leadership positions from pharmaceutical, medical sales, education, insurance, real estate, telemarketing, mortgages, network marketing, home health and hospice. In corporate America as well an in entrepreneurship, Nichelle has been tagged the negotiator and the deal closer.

In her spare time when she is not doing business (rarely), Nichelle enjoys meeting new people, traveling, thrifting, home decorating, eating fine foods, cooking, wine tasting, writing, attending her son's basketball games and rehabbing houses. Learn more about Nichelle at **The Start Up CEO** or her **website**. She's also on **Instagram** as well as **YouTube**. Sign up for her **mailing list** for business tips, inspiration and motivation. You can also subscribe to **The People Connect Podcast** for business tips, inspiration and motivation.

www.ingramcontent.com/pod-product-compliance
Lightning Source LLC
Chambersburg PA
CBHW071202220526
45468CB00003B/1124